THE POCKET LIBRARY OF GREAT ART

*Plate 1.* PICASSO IN ·1901. *Drawing by Ramón Casas*
*Courtesy The Museum of Modern Art, New York*

PABLO

# PICASSO

*Blue and Rose Periods*

*text by*

WILLIAM S. LIEBERMAN

*Curator of Prints*
*The Museum of Modern Art, New York*

*published by* HARRY N. ABRAMS, INC., *in association*
*with* POCKET BOOKS, INC., *New York*

FOR MARGA AND ALFRED

*On the cover
detail of* BOY WITH A PIPE *(plate 31)*

*Plate 2.* THE WATERING PLACE. *1905. Pencil, 11¼ x 17½"*
*Collection Walter P. Chrysler, Jr., New York*

At the age of twenty-five, when Picasso finished the last painting in this book, he had already produced a body of work which in quality and quantity few artists achieve in a lifetime. Today, half a century later, these early paintings remain the most popular of his work of any period.

Pablo Picasso was born in 1881 in Malaga on the southern Mediterranean coast of Spain. His father, a painter of Basque origin, was a civic instructor of drawing, first at Malaga and, after 1891, at Corunna where the northern tip of Galicia points into the Atlantic.

Picasso's formal studies were irregular. An indifferent student with no scholastic aptitude, he was far more interested in the materials of his father's studio. At the age of twelve he drew competent renditions of plaster casts and began his first serious attempts at painting.

In 1895, just before his fifteenth birthday, the family moved to Barcelona where his father had been appointed to the School of Fine Arts. The young Picasso attended the same academy and brilliantly passed the entrance examinations to advanced classes. This prodigious performance was repeated the following year at the School of Fine Arts in Madrid where Picasso spent the winter of 1897.

Proud of its cultural tradition as the capital of Catalonia, Barcelona by its geographic location was receptive to ideas and influences from the rest of Europe. Many of her painters and writers travelled to France and Germany and, at home, books and periodicals spread the self-conscious aesthetic of the *fin de siècle* and the decorative style of the *art nouveau*. Intellectually, Barcelona was the most cosmopolitan city of Spain.

Picasso's return to Barcelona in 1898 coincided with the opening of a restaurant and cabaret called in Catalan *Els 4 Gats* (The Four Cats). Modeled on the *brasseries* of Paris, the *4 Gats* attracted the avant-garde of the city. In an atmosphere of lively bohemia Picasso met poets, collectors, critics, and, most important, other artists. His startling precocity compensated for any difference in age, and, today, he remains faithful to several of these early friendships.

The most prominent painter to frequent the *4 Gats* was Ramón Casas, a successful portraitist and a fashionable figure about Barcelona. Casas had brought from Paris a knowledge of the French Impressionists and an appreciation of the draftsmanship of Carrière, Steinlen, and Toulouse-Lautrec, the three contemporary painters who most influenced the early Picasso.

In 1900 Picasso was nineteen. He had won prizes at exhibitions in Malaga and Madrid. He has always disliked contributing to group exhibitions, however, and was

*Plate 3.* SEATED GIRL. *1895. Oil, 29½ x 20". Owned by the artist*

*Plate 4.* ROSES. *1898. Oil, 14¼ x 16¾"*

*Collection Mrs. Potter Palmer, Chicago*

delighted that a one-man show of his portrait drawings was held at the *4 Gats*. He could have remained in Barcelona where his work had been remarked and even reproduced, but the intellectual stimulus that dictated the atmosphere of the *4 Gats* came from beyond the Pyrenees. In October he set out for Paris with Carlos Casagemas, a close friend with whom he shared a studio.

The trip to Paris was short, and the only major painting of this first visit is the *Moulin de la Galette* (plate 12). Casagemas drank, fell in love, and brooded suicide. Picasso grew concerned and in December they returned to Spain to spend Christmas with his family. The two young men celebrated New Year's of 1901 in Malaga, but, even for Picasso, Casagemas proved too strenuous a companion. Picasso left for Madrid, Casagemas returned to Paris.

In Madrid, Picasso and the writer Francisco A. de Soler started a monthly magazine *Arte Joven,* a youthful answer to *Pel & Ploma,* a periodical sponsored in Barcelona by Ramón Casas. Although the magazine lasted only five issues, it gave the young artist the assurance of seeing his work published. Another review—to be called *Madrid*—was planned, but the project did not materialize and Picasso went home to Barcelona.

Under the auspices of Casas, against whom he seems posed in friendly rivalry, Picasso held an exhibition of pastels and drawings at the Salon Parés. He stayed in Barcelona less than a month and in May returned to Paris.

Soon after his arrival Ambroise Vollard showed a few of his paintings in a small exhibition that attracted little notice. Picasso remained in Paris half a year. For a while his subjects continued to be the same—still lifes, street scenes, the night life of cabarets and music halls. But gradually his free adaptation of Impressionism became disciplined by more stylized compositions in flat patterns.

In the last months of 1901 his painting grew increasingly introspective. Casagemas had committed suicide, and one of the first compositions in this new style was a large

*Plate 5.* THE ARTIST'S SISTER. *1899. Oil, 59 x 39½"*
*Owned by the artist*

*Plate 6.* PARIS STREET. *1900. Oil, 18½ x 26"*
*San Francisco Museum of Art*

burial scene commemorating his death. When the poet
Jaime Sabartés, another friend from Barcelona, arrived in
Paris in the autumn, he was astonished at the recent change
in Picasso's work. The lively street scenes and vivid por-
traits had given way to the succession of played-out prosti-
tutes and sad mothers who introduce the "blue period."

In January 1902 Picasso returned to Barcelona and
shared a studio with the painter Rocarol. He visited Paris
for a third time briefly in November, but during most of
1902 and all of the succeeding year remained in Spain.
The brooding melancholy of the blue period persisted over
three years. The distortions of his drawing expressed sadness and despair. His themes were mournful—the sick,
the aged, the hungry, and the blind. Never again was his
painting to remain so somber for so long.

Various explanations for the blue period have been of-

*Plate 7.* THE UPPER DECK. *1901. Oil, 19⅛ x 25¼"*
*The Art Institute of Chicago (Mr. and Mrs. L. L. Coburn Collection)*

fered, some of them extraordinary. Whatever the reason, and the answer is in Picasso himself, the color blue was ideally suited to his anguished themes. These paintings are by a young man not yet twenty-five, an artist mature beyond his years who lives in poverty and has yet to discover happiness or success. The forlorn characters may reflect a *fin de siècle* desperation, but Picasso never comments on the social implications inherent in his subjects.

In the spring of 1904 Picasso settled permanently in Paris. He lived on Montmartre in a rambling tenement called by the painters and poets who roomed in it the *bateau lavoir*—the floating laundry. During the following months the insistent pathos of the blue period gradually disappeared. Many mannerisms persist, but the pose of the figures became less postured and the monochrome of blue less dominant. The most obvious change in his paintings of 1905 appeared in a new cast of characters—acrobats, jugglers, and clowns. Over and over again he drew these performers who evoke a romantic nostalgia for the *cirque forain*. They are presented in couples or in groups, not singly as were the lonely and destitute figures of the blue period.

Picasso intended to feature the saltimbanques in two large figure compositions. The first, a camp of itinerant circus folk, was never executed but is outlined in several prints and drawings (plate 42). The second is *The Saltimbanques* (plates 26–30), seven and a half feet wide, the largest canvas of Picasso's first decade as a painter.

In the latter half of 1905 Picasso abandoned his sensitive, sentimental characterizations for a more objective point of view. He planned a third large picture but, again, the painting was never begun. The composition, however, is laid out in several preliminary studies and details (plates 2, 39 & 43). Nude horsemen and their four mounts gather at a watering place. The idyllic theme reveals the nourishing interest in the classic ideal which will run throughout Picasso's career.

This first classic style is often described as the "rose period." Paintings such as *Boy with a Pipe* (plate 31) exploit a shade of terra-cotta pink which a year later in *La Toilette* became as pervasive as the former blue.

The tranquillity and restraint of the rose period reflects the happier circumstances of his personal life. In 1904, while at work on the etching reproduced on plate 36, Picasso had met Fernande Olivier. They lived together for several years and her statuesque beauty graces many of his paintings. Their life was often stormy—Picasso is domineering and wilful—but for the first time he settled down to daily domesticity. The tense, neurotic, and sometimes morbid undertones of much of his earlier painting vanished before the calm and relaxation of the rose period. A slight improvement in his finances further stabilized his

*Plate 8.* THE MOTHER. *1901. Oil, 29½ x 20¼"*
*City Art Museum, St. Louis*

routine of living. His work achieved a measure of recognition; sales, although often forced, were more frequent.

In Paris, as in Spain, many of his acquaintances were writers. Picasso has always attracted the literary, and they are often his best propagandists. Although he continued to see many Catalans in Paris, his closest friends were the poets Max Jacob and Guillaume Apollinaire.

Through Henri Roché, Picasso met two Americans, Leo Stein and his sister Gertrude. By the standards of Montmartre, the Steins were extremely wealthy, and Leo had begun to assemble an important collection of modern art. The Steins became his first important patrons. They introduced his work to other Americans and Picasso himself to other artists.

Although Gertrude Stein perhaps never understood Picasso as an artistic personality, she was quick to realize the vitality and drive of his ambition. During the winter and spring of 1906 she sat for her portrait (plate 33). Picasso seldom works continuously from a model; he grew dissatisfied and left the face unfinished. After a summer with Fernande in the Spanish Pyrenees, he returned to Paris and painted in the head. The mask-like face suggests a radical redirection in his art which his next paintings will rapidly confirm. As an author Gertrude Stein grew to consider her writings as a parallel to Picasso's achievement as a painter. Thirty years later, she said of her portrait: "For me, it is I, and it is the only reproduction of me which is always I, for me."

The paintings reproduced on the following pages were done within a period of six years from 1900 through 1906. They trace the development and increasing stylization of the blue period, then its transition to a broader and less mannered method of painting. These early works will always have great appeal. They give little indication, however, that Picasso was to become the prime innovator, the most important (and the most controversial) painter of our time.

# COLOR PLATES

PLATE 9

## SELF-PORTRAIT

*Painted 1901. Oil, 20¼ x 12½"*
*Collection Mr. & Mrs. John Hay Whitney,*
*New York*

Picasso cut short his first visit to Paris to
spend the winter in Madrid and Barcelona. His stay in Spain confirmed his
ambition and served as a catalyst to his
art. This self-portrait and five pictures
reproduced on the following pages were
painted upon his return to Paris. This
second visit lasted six months, and within
so short a time he painted some seventy
canvases. These paintings reveal many
influences and no single direction. They
are, however, the accomplishment of a
mature artist.

The vivid portrait is a virtuoso performance. Picasso's analysis of himself is
summary and bold. He leaves no distance
between himself and the spectator.
Audacious, impetuous, and alert, his gaze
is compelling and direct.

PLATE 10

# THE ABSINTHE DRINKER

*Painted 1901. Oil, 30⅜ x 26⅜"*
*Collection Mr. & Mrs. John Hay Whitney,*
*New York*

The absinthe drinker belongs to the dere-
lict fringe of the city. She sits alone. Her
hair is unkempt, her sleeves too tight. A
knitted shawl covers her shoulders. In the
background, beyond the cafe terrace,
night obscures shadowy figures as they
pass in the street.

The colors are rich and varied. But
Picasso's treatment has little compassion.
The woman grasps a lump of sugar and
raises it to her glass of absinthe. The claw
of a hand seems as predatory as her
pointed features.

This painting formerly belonged to the
American composer George Gershwin.

PLATE 11

OLD WOMAN

*Painted 1901. Oil, 26½ x 20½"*
*Philadelphia Museum of Art*
*(Louise and Walter Arensberg Coll.)*

The *Old Woman* shows a lively adaptation of Impressionist brushwork. The spots of color are bright, and Picasso models his rapid draftsmanship on the quick character sketches of Toulouse-Lautrec. Over-rouged and over-used, the old hag cackles the laughter of the depraved or insane.

Picasso, again like Lautrec, finds inspiration in the night life of Paris, its streets and cabarets. The picture on the next pages (plate 12) was painted a few months earlier. The most important painting of his first trip to Paris, it offers a sultry view of the Moulin de la Galette so lovingly painted by Renoir, with whom Picasso invites comparison.

*Plate 12.* LE MOULIN DE LA GALETTE. *Painted 1900. Oil, 35¼ x 45¾"*

PLATE 13

# HARLEQUIN

*Painted 1901. Oil, 31½ x 23¼"*
*Collection Mr. and Mrs. Henry Clifford,*
*Radnor, Pennsylvania*

Picasso alternated briefly between two
styles. The *Old Woman* and the *Absinthe
Drinker* were lustily painted in rapid
brush strokes. The composition of the
*Harlequin* is more formal, however, and
the flat, poster-like effect typical of several paintings of 1901.

Picasso exploits the decorative possi-
bilities of the design. The squares of the
harlequin's tights are contained within
the reverse "S" formed by his body. The
banquette isolates the seated figure, and
this broad horizontal is in turn relieved
by the bold pattern of the wallpaper. At
the right, a container of matches balances
the composition and repeats the round-
ness of the table. The *Harlequin* intro-
duces for the first time a character who
will appear frequently in Picasso's circus
paintings of 1905.

PLATE 14

## THE GOURMET

*Painted 1901. Oil, 36 x 27"*
*Chester Dale Collection, New York*

As Picasso's ability to speak French in-
creased, the circle of his friends widened.
The most devoted of his new companions
in Paris was the poet Max Jacob, whom
he met at Ambroise Vollard's crowded
gallery on the rue Laffitte. Vollard, already launched as a dealer and publisher,
arranged an exhibition of Picasso's paintings.

*The Gourmet,* painted shortly after his
arrival, was included in his first Paris
exhibition. It is an ingratiating anecdote,
an appealing and somewhat saccharine
prelude to more somber works. The
rhythmic silhouettes of the larger areas
suggest a debt to Gauguin as well as to
the curvilinear style of the *art nouveau.*
The color blue is increasingly pervasive.

PLATES 15 & 16

## THE BLUE ROOM

*Painted 1901. Oil, 20 x 24½"*
*Phillips Collection, Washington, D.C.*

The composition of *The Blue Room* is not
yet characteristic of the blue period. It is
a horizontal rather than a vertical picture,
an interior rather than a study of a single
figure. The receding perspective is, for
Picasso, extremely naturalistically de-
fined. The paint itself is thickly applied
and, as in the *Harlequin* and *The Gourmet,* heavy touches of white relieve the
incipient monochrome of blue.

The room is Picasso's own. Posted on
the wall is Toulouse-Lautrec's large litho-
graph of May Milton. The bed is unmade,
and a woman takes her morning bath.
The atmosphere is intimate and informal.
There is no feeling of strain or tension
such as fevers *La Vie,* the next painting
and Picasso's most ambitious work of the
blue period.

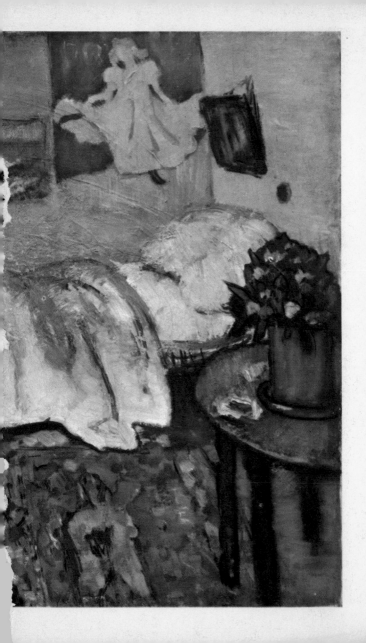

PLATE 17

## LA VIE

*Painted 1903. Oil, 77⅜ x 50⅞"*
*The Cleveland Museum of Art*
*(Gift of Hanna Fund)*

Allegory is obviously intended, but, as so
often with Picasso, the meaning remains
personal and eludes exact definition. The
awkwardly posed couple at the left derive
from studies of a man and woman locked
in an embrace. Here, however, their union
seems protective rather than sensual. The
man points to an older woman who
cradles a sleeping baby. In contrast to the
naked and self-conscious couple, the
heavily draped figure appears aloof and
statuesque. In the background two paintings underscore the mood of sadness—
above, a man clings to a woman; below,
the same figure crouches in despair.

Critics suggest that this picture called
"Life" describes the three ages of man.
More probably its meaning lies in unreal-
ized parenthood. Its very ambiguity suggests Picasso's own state of mind.

PLATE 18

## THE OLD GUITARIST

*Painted 1903. Oil, 47¾ x 32½"*
*The Art Institute of Chicago (Helen Birch
Bartlett Memorial Collection)*

The man bent over his guitar,
A shearsman of sorts. The day was green.

They said, "You have a blue guitar,
You do not play things as they are."

The man replied, "Things as they are
Are changed upon the blue guitar . . ."
                    —WALLACE STEVENS

This painting of a blind, wailing guitarist
summarizes the extremes of the blue period. The expressive distortions, reminis-
cent of El Greco and certain Romanesque
sculptures, have become so exaggerated
that they seem mannered. Like the win-
dow, whose glimpse of sky silhouettes the
bent head, the rectangle of the picture
emphasizes the angular and contorted
pose.

PLATE 19

# BLIND MAN'S MEAL

*Painted 1903. Oil, 37½ x 37¼"*
*The Metropolitan Museum of Art*
*(Gift of Mr. and Mrs. Ira Haupt)*

In Paris and in Barcelona Picasso was desperately poor. He often went hungry, and the frequent appearance of food and drink in his early work is revealing as a mirror of the vicissitudes of his own life. Over and over again he painted men and women seated at a table. Food, if any, is a bowl of gruel or a crust of bread; drink, a bottle of wine or a glass of absinthe.

The composition of the *Blind Man's Meal* is characteristic — a single figure against a simple background fills the picture. The repast is frugal but furnishes Picasso with the materials for a still life.

PLATE 20

# WOMAN IRONING

*Painted 1904. Oil, 46⅛ x 29⅛"*
*Collection Mr. and Mrs. Justin K. Thann-*
*hauser, New York*

The brooding melancholy of the blue pe-
riod endured for more than three years.
His good friend, the poet and novelist
Jaime Sabartes, recalls that at this time
Picasso believed that art "emanates from
sadness and pain."

The frailty of the laundress is under-
lined by the feeling of weight as she
presses down upon the iron. The tumbling
strands of hair repeat the movement, and
the effort of her body is emphasized by
its distortion.

Compare the *Woman Ironing* with the
*Old Guitarist* (plate 18). In both paintings the head and raised shoulder appear
in the same position. The blind guitarist
wails a chant of sorrow. The woman,
however, seems less wretched and the
wan, smiling face peculiarly resigned to
the drudgery of her task.

PLATES 21 & 22

## THE ACTOR
*Painted 1904–05. Oil, 77¼ x 45⅛"*
*The Metropolitan Museum of Art, N. Y.*

*The Actor* is almost life size. The sentimental pathos has for a moment disappeared. And the pervasive monochrome
of blue surrenders to a palette still sub-
dued but different in tonality.

In comparison with the old guitarist or
the woman ironing, the figure is less
cramped within the frame of the picture
and moves freely in the space around it.
The sinuous turns of the arms, torso, and
legs differ from the angular and flat distortions of the previous months. The at-
tenuations are graced by a Gothic ele-
gance which will characterize Picasso's
draftsmanship during the next year.

The actor takes position on an empty
stage before the prompter's box. In the
background the stage apron rises abruptly
to meet the proscenium wing. The perspective is daring, but the composition
lacks complete integration.

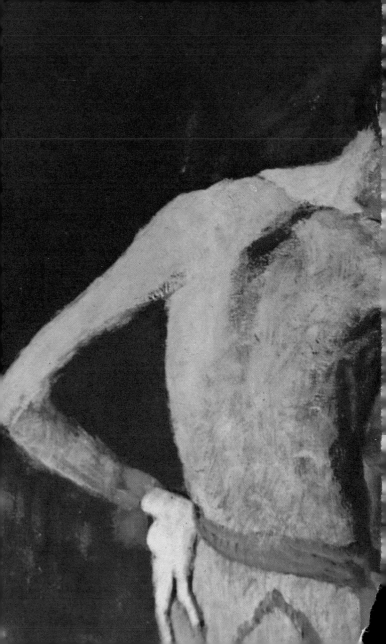

PLATE 23

## TWO SALTIMBANQUES WITH A DOG

*Painted 1905. Gouache, 41½ x 29½"*
*Collection Wright Ludington, Santa Bar-*
*bara, California*

Despair gradually gave way to a mood still melancholy but more tender. In 1905 the blind beggars and woeful women of the blue period were replaced by a new cast of characters—saltimbanques and mountebanks, the gypsies of the theater.

These two adolescents are not on stage —the curtain has fallen, the audience has gone—but two weary travellers at the outskirts of town. The taller boy carries a pack. The colors of his lozenged tights, muted as they seem, are more varied than those of any costume of the blue period. The younger boy, his beardless face perversely aged beyond his actual years, touches a gentle mongrel dog, such as Picasso himself owned.

PLATE 24

# THE HARLEQUIN'S FAMILY

*Painted 1905. Watercolor, 23 x 17¼"*
*Collection Mrs. Sam A. Lewisohn, N.Y.*

With Max Jacob and other friends Picasso was a weekly visitor to the Cirque Medrano on Montmartre. The acrobats and circus performers intrigued his imagination, and around them he invented a life completely divorced from their actual existence in the theater.

Picasso develops the story of his saltimbanques in detail. He frequently presents them in the intimacy of their daily life. *The Harlequin's Family* is a genre scene, a glimpse of domestic routine. The father holds the child as the mother arranges her hair into an upswept chignon. The theme of a woman before a mirror will be constantly repeated in Picasso's art. Here, his treatment is an informal as his method—delicate drawing lightly brushed with watercolor.

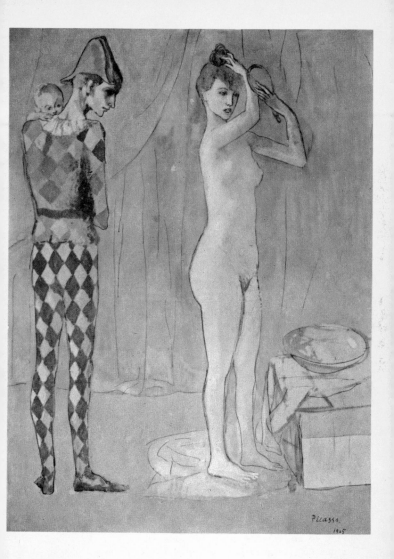

Picasso
1905

PLATE 25

# TWO SALTIMBANQUES
*1905. Pastel, 27½ x 20½"*
*Collection Stephen C. Clark, New York*

This pastel has the spontaneity and charm
of a rapid sketch. It is a modest work,
casual and unpretentious. It offers a fresh
variation on the theme of the two saltimbanques, a boy and an older man. There
is no suggestion of sadness and, in comparison with the painting reproduced on
plate 23, there is little attenuation in the
treatment of the figures.

The source of light is not the day but
an artificial illumination from the right.
The costumes and the chiaroscuro of the
drawing also contribute to a sense of the
theater. The brown tint of the paper itself supplies a curtain against which
the changing values of blue and pink
gracefully complement each other.

PLATES 26 & 27

## THE SALTIMBANQUES

*Painted 1905. Oil, 84 x 90⅜"*
*National Gallery of Art, Washington,*
*D.C. (Chester Dale Collection, Loan)*

Every few years Picasso concentrates into
one large painting the problems of an
entire period of work. The composition
of *The Saltimbanques* was perhaps sug-
gested by Manet's painting of an old
musician seated out-of-doors and sur-
rounded by five figures, three of them
children. The preliminary studies differ
considerably from the finished picture,
and while at work on the canvas itself,
Picasso changed the composition several
times. In the final painting, as the detail
reveals, the profile of the harlequin at
the left has been altered to suggest a self-
portrait of the artist.

On the next pages appear three addi-
tional details of *The Saltimbanques.*

PLATES 28, 29 & 30

## THE SALTIMBANQUES
details of plate 27

*Painted 1905. Oil, 84 x 90⅜"*
*National Gallery of Art, Washington,*
*D.C. (Chester Dale Collection, Loan)*

*The Saltimbanques* gathers together performers already presented in other works
of the circus period. This may explain
why the figures seem posed, static, and
curiously independent of each other. The
seated lady at the right bears no psycho-
logical relationship to any of the other
characters. Indeed, she was the subject
for a separate painting. The other details
juxtapose two children—the girl with a
flower basket and the little boy in oriental
costume.

If various elements of the painting
seem unresolved, it may be this very in-
completeness that contributes an air of
expectancy, a suggestion of mystery and
romance. *The Saltimbanques* inspired the
German poet Rainer Maria Rilke to com-
pose the fifth of his *Duino Elegies*—"But
tell me, who *are* they, these acrobats,
even a little more fleeting than we our-
selves." Have they just arrived? Are they
about to depart? The picture invites the
spectator to finish its story.

PLATE 31

BOY WITH A PIPE
*Painted 1905. Oil, 39 x 31"*
*Collection Mr. & Mrs. John Hay Whitney,*
*New York*

In the latter half of 1905 Picasso abandoned his sensitive and often introspective
characterizations of saltimbanques. He
was briefly interested in sculpture and,
after a short trip to Holland during the
summer, his painting became more objective. Even in the *Boy with a Pipe,* so
closely related to the pictures of circus
performers, Picasso's attitude seems more
detached. The face is that of the taller
boy in the painting reproduced on plate
23, but Picasso's interest is formal rather
than narrative, and the backdrop of
painted flowers throws the figures into
bold relief.

    *Boy with a Pipe* is one of the first paint-
ings of the rose period.

PLATE 32

## LA TOILETTE

*Painted 1906. Oil, 59½ x 39½"*
*Albright Art Gallery, Buffalo*

The pose of the two women at the right might have been adapted from some red-figured Greek vase of the fifth century. The resemblance is not accidental. Over and over again Picasso returns to the breadth and poise of a classic style in themes that seem timeless and remote.

The broadly painted, relaxed, and substantially modeled nude of *La Toilette* offers a vivid contrast to the fragile, almost emaciated nudes of *La Vie* or *The Harlequin's Family*. The drawing is vigorous rather than delicate, the tranquil pose serene.

The picture was probably painted in Gosol in the Spanish Pyrenees. It is one of a series of nudes which, no matter how idealized, remain spontaneous and unacademic.

PLATE 33

## GERTRUDE STEIN

*Painted 1906. Oil, 39¼ x 32"*
*The Metropolitan Museum of Art, N.Y.*

The severely modeled face offers a startling contrast to the rest of the painting.
In her *Autobiography of Alice B. Toklas,*
Gertrude Stein describes why. "Picasso
sat very tight on his chair and very close
to his canvas and on a very small palette
which was of a uniform brown gray color,
mixed some more brown gray and the
painting began. This was the first of some
eighty or ninety sittings. . . .

"All of a sudden one day Picasso
painted out the whole head. I can't see
you any longer when I look, he said
irritably. And so the picture was left
like that. . . .

"The day he returned from Spain
Picasso sat down and out of his head
painted the head without having seen
Gertrude Stein again. . . .

"Yes, he said, everybody says she does
not look like it but that does not make
any difference, she will, he said."

*Plate 34. THE PAINTER ROCAROL. 1899. Crayon and watercolor, 20½ x 12⅞", Fogg Museum of Art, Cambridge, Mass.*

*Plate 35.* BIBI, THE DOWN-AND-OUT. *1901. Pencil, 17⅛ x 11⅜"*
*Collection Walter P. Chrysler, Jr., New York*

*Plate 36.* THE FRUGAL REPAST. *1904. Etching, 18¼ x 14¾"*
*Museum of Modern Art, N. Y. (Gift of Mrs. John D. Rockefeller, Jr.)*